RISE
ABOVE
REJECTION

Exposing the "little girl" in me

To David,

Continue to Rise!

Love,

Dr. [signature]

Dr. Valerie Martin-Stewart

Dr. Valerie Martin-Stewart
Founder and Executive Director of
Taking It By Force Outreach Ministries
Inc.

www.valeriemstewart.com
vstewart@knology.net

Photos and cover design by
Shelly Williams

Printed in the U.S.A.

CONTENTS

DEDICATIONS

I dedicate this book to God, Jesus, and the Holy Spirit for working and moving awesomely in my life!

Secondly, I dedicate this book to my loving Mother, *Louise Martin-Pope*, who is deceased but one day I shall see her again. It's through her great provision and protection that this book has come about. However, my perception at four years old caused my little head and heart to feel rejection. Thanks be to God, it's all right now!

Thirdly, I dedicate this book to my siblings *Hervie Eugene (Gene), Joyce Ann, Thomas Lee, Bruce Leon, Beverly Ann, Tawanda Renee (Renee) and my loving daughter, Paris Marie* for the love, the laughter, and the inspirations each of you have given to me throughout my life! I love you all in a very special way!

Fourthly, I dedicate this book to my dear *Aunt Annie* and *Uncle Joe* who have taken my siblings and me into their homes and nurtured us, leading and guiding us in the ways of *life*. I learned that fullness of life is only found in Jesus! You gave us Jesus and now I realize because of getting Him, I can have everything else, according to St. Matthew 6:33! Thanks to both of you, and I am forever grateful to you!

Fifthly, I dedicate this book to Dr. Wade Kornegay, a retired Research Scientist Director of Lincoln Laboratory of Massachusetts Institute of Technology and a good friend of mine, who taught me to be good to myself. He often said "People will treat you the way they see you treating yourself and if you don't be good to yourself, neither will others."

Sixthly, I dedicate this book to Sandra Blue, Dr. Claudette Owens, Patricia Jefferson, Vairy Spencer, Gloria Flowers, and all of the ladies at Space and Missile Defense Command (SMDC) in Huntsville, AL where I was once employed. Each of you have pushed and encouraged me during some of my darkest days. I love you and thank each of my sisters for the "push."

Lastly, I dedicate this book to each and every reader who has ever experienced any form of rejection. I dedicate this book to you, having a revelation from God that as you read this book, you *will* have clarity of your own *root* of rejection. Not only that, but your heart will experience the perfect and divine love of our Father working out your pain. Know that there *is* a beginning place of your rejection whether it was the wrong perception, actual or factual.

ACKNOWLEDGEMENTS

I want to give special thanks to Dr. Henry Bradford, a professor and dear friend of mine who took the time, at a very short notice, to edit my work. I praise God for your wisdom, knowledge, and willingness to share your God-given talents. I love you and truly thank you!

I want to particularly give special recognition to Elder Bobby and Amy Sledge (Pastor of Victory World Outreach Ministries in Huntsville, AL) and the church family for being there for me and believing in me! I thank you Elder Sledge for over and over again, allowing God to use you to speak awesome, <u>manifested,</u> prophetic *words of life* into my soul. Thank you for "calling" out the "little girl" in Water Valley, MS in November 2007. For that day, I was *totally* delivered and set free from over 30+ years of battling with the spirit of rejection. I love you all so much and thank God for bringing us together to do KINGDOM work and not just CHURCH work!

I must give thanks to the Victory World Outreach praise team for singing and being on FIRE (FYE) for God Sunday after Sunday!!! Truly, you lifted my very spirit from depths of depression and ushered me right into the presence of the Almighty God!!! I thank you and love each of you!!! Stay on FYE for JESUS!!!

To all of you who have asked me, "When Val, are you going to *stop* achieving or when will you reach your maximum?" I can only share with each of you what pierces my heart. Every time I attempt to procrastinate, become slothful and *rest* in my comfort zone, I hear these words: "For unto whomsoever much is given, of him shall be much required." (Luke 12:48b) Therefore, I can't emphasize enough to each of you the dangers of shrinking and comparing yourself to others. There are others connected to your destiny therefore, you must arrive there quickly and safely.

FOREWORD

One of my favorite teacher and authors is Evangelist Joyce Meyer. In the foreword of her book on rejection entitled "The Root of Rejection" she wrote these words:

"Rejection starts as a seed planted in our lives through various things that happen to us. God said his people should become trees of righteousness (Isaiah 61:3, KJV). Trees have roots, and roots determine fruit! Rotten fruit comes from rotten roots and good fruit comes from good roots. Whatever we are rooted in will determine the fruit in our lives."

When I first saw and heard of Joyce Meyer's book on rejection some years ago, I immediately became interested and knew I needed to read it. I purchased it and to this day I have yet to complete reading it. Why? Because as I sat to read it, I heard the Holy Spirit say unto me that I had my own book concerning rejection inside of me that needed to be told. I thought, really! Still eager to read Joyce's story, I tried reading further but to no avail. I finally understood. I knew God was telling me to tune into Him and write my own story. At that time, I just didn't know which story. A few years later, in a very strange way, God gave me my own book on rejection even though I *thought* it was *only* a divine revelation and information for *my* knowing *only*.

So, where do I start? How do I write and explain a divine revelation from the Holy Spirit given unto to me at a time when I was feeling extremely low, struggling with voices telling me to end my life? I could not have known this very detailed information about myself from a spiritual aspect without the Holy Spirit's direct insight.

So, understand that the first book was written out of my logic and carnal awareness of what I wanted to say or project, no doubt with the Holy Spirit's guidance. The pain I was acquainted with oh so well. However, this book is written out of an overwhelming encounter with the devil, the Holy Spirit and myself on Interstate 65 headed north to Nashville in October 2003. The divine revelation is about me. Not the adult Val, but the "little girl" that has been living on the inside of me and often manifested herself *through* the adult Val.

I must admit. I'm r-e-a-l nervous about this book, yet relieved, and I shall explain the two. Nervous, because this book makes me sound and look as though there's a real war going on in my spirit. I'm talking of a serious split personality. Relieved, because I understand myself now and so many of the problems I've had in relationships with family, friends, bosses, coaches, boyfriends and even in my previous marriage. I, like everyone, desire to appear stable, sure of myself and look sane to the world. But this book does just the opposite in my view. It's revealing...very revealing. It's revealing enough to leave any reader questioning my stability.

It's not easy to lay your feelings, emotions, and wounds on the line only for those who are so quick to judge, for those who "think" they are alright, and those who believe you and I are the ones who need help, not them, size you up wrongly.

The thought that they will perhaps get hold of this book and make even stronger, deeper, and outright untruths about me is somewhat scary. However, because I am free, hallelujah, since the Son has set me free, I'm not afraid to share perhaps what you will never understand and may be too fearful to tell about your own life. Ralph Ellison said it this way, "When I discover who I am, I'll be free." Freedom is something I've longed for *all* of my life. One of my favorite poems published in my first book is entitled, "I Want To Be Free."

I've never physically been locked behind bars so know that this freedom is desired *from within.* I've longed to be free of what people will think of me. I've longed to express myself in a positive manner without fear. I've longed to get delivered and break free of me!!! For I understand and believe God's Word that says "my worse enemy is in *my own house.*" I "house" all of my emotions, feelings, struggles and setbacks. We all would be so much better if we stopped blaming others for the shape and condition of our own lives. We must take some responsibility if we plan to *rise* and be effective at any level.

I'm very open in my speech, but very introverted in my dealings with mankind. "Complex" is just one of the many words that some have used to describe me. And of all the words, I agree with this one the most. I definitely see, feel, and know that I am real complex; almost as complex as the Pythagorean Theorem used to be unto me.

Yet I've learned to embrace my uniqueness and I'm finally learning how to truly love myself, and be free to express myself regardless without fearing what anybody will think. Sounds arrogant to you? Let me tell you...that's shear freedom for me because all of my life I've burdened myself and lived with the haunting thought of "what will people think?" It's devastating, torturing and an outright prison sentence for anyone who longs to be free for as long as I have. Writing to me is freedom! I realize I don't have to do it your way or anyone's way and that I'm still all right. I've learned that I can be myself with myself and never try to fool myself. For that truly isn't love, but inadvertent hate messages sent unto myself.

As I reflect on the many times I *shrunk* in life trying to "fit in" with others while making myself very miserable pains me. Not wanting to be rejected had devastating blows on my actions. God used my basketball career to demonstrate unto me how I've shrunk in almost every setting. He told me that deep within, I knew I could easily go out and score 20+ points most nights, but I didn't because I wanted to please my team mates who were telling me not to score all the points and let them score.

I did and I typically only scored when I stole the ball (because I was quick and could anticipate where the ball was going next). I feared their rejection. I was a great passer, so I thrived on passing the ball and making them look good. I shrunk on the teams and I shrunk in the classroom at times (by not scoring my highest on test) when my peers made statements like, "I know Val studied hard and is going to make an "A", right Val?"

I wanted to prove to them I wasn't that smart, while knowing all the answers sometime, but I intentionally marked some wrong.

However, I can't stress enough of how "trying to fit in" has haunted me all of my life which caused me to take extreme measure. Oh, how I cherish the words of Nelson Mandela. Excerpts from one of his speeches said, "Our deepest fear is not that we are inadequate; our deepest fear is that we are powerful beyond measure. It is our light, not our darkness that most frightens us. Your playing small does not serve the world. As we are liberated from our own fears, we automatically liberate those around us. As we let our own light shine, we unconsciously give people the permission to do the same."

Whenever I read his speech in its entirety, I'm instantaneously motivated and driven from within like you wouldn't believe!!! I believe that we are born with internal resources that are needed to succeed but they must be tapped into.

I've shed many tears, relived, and revisited much of my pain while attempting to write this book. Therefore, I want to express to my family, particularly my siblings, that I've said nor written anything to intentionally offend you. My intentions solely are to write my story and share my first-hand experience with rejection. I strongly believe that each reader who has dealt with any form of rejection will experience healing as you read this book.

I've struggled, strained and lived with rejection for more than 32 years of my life. I was 37 years old when this revelation took place. I'm 40 now. Yes, it's been a long struggle. However, God has decided enough is enough. I must write my story and share it so that many others will know that they are not alone and they too can overcome the devastating feelings of rejection.

I also want to emphatically make another fact known. I loved my mother, Louise Martin-Pope, with every part of my being. She's deceased now. And I know she loved me with every sinew of her body. So, don't read anything into the things I will share. What I feel is all written in plain form and understanding. So, realize that this is not a "hate" message about my Mom. No, it's actually all about love. You see, in order for me to be able to finally write my story reveals I've experienced great love. Love from family, friends, but most of all from God.

God has taught me that before I can be used greatly, I may have to be wounded deeply. He's real concerned about each of us being healed from the inside out. He wants us to stop covering our pain with makeup, phony smiles, pretty clothes, inflated egos, jokes, jobs, alcohol, drugs, and insecure relationships.

He wants us to know the truth about ourselves, our situations, our families, and the "whys" of life that we so often ask. However, in order to get *healed,* we must be willing to allow God to *reveal* all of those things we have purposely *concealed.* None of this has come without a struggle for healing is truly a <u>process</u> (a word I used to despise) unless God decides to perform a supernatural miracle. We do know He's very much able and capable of doing just that! Frederick Douglas said, "If there is no struggle, there is no progress." I thank God for *every* struggle!

A READER'S COMMENTS

If an individual never has been bothered, bewildered, or burdened with any emotional restraints, loneliness, rejection, fears and incessant tears, such a person might have difficulty understanding this author's vivid recollections.

In most day-to-day human relations it is rather easy to graciously accept and abide by the delightful words, which come from the legacy of the gifted writer of Proverbs in Holy Scripture. The words from Proverbs 15:13a declare that "A merry heart maketh a cheerful countenance" but unfortunately, not every human being can appropriate that challenging declaration. For quite an extended time in her life the author of this book, Valerie Martin-Stewart, surely could not. Even with so many laudable accomplishments and times of intellectual achievement in her life and successful athletic awards, still her emotional stress remained. However, it is by her overcoming many emotional trials that serious readers will find extremely high hope. The truth is that she became greatly victorious amidst it all because of an increasingly stronger and more steadfast relationship with God and His only Son, Jesus Christ. With that significant relationship Doctor Stewart has been empowered to become emotionally transparent through her writing. In an undisguised and unsophisticated manner she has been inspired to give hope for relief and release to others in their distress through the unconditional love of God with which she has been tremendously blessed. The intended wish here is that those who can identify with her rough times and perplexing experiences can choose to move towards the realization of full victory.

Thomas A. Dorsey, a writer of much gospel music, literally opened the closed door for so many troubled people. He speaks powerfully, confidently and truthfully as a man who just happens to be a black American. He said:

> Like a ship that's toss'd and driven,
> battered by an angry sea,

When the storms of life are raging
and their fury falls on me,

I wonder what I have done that
makes this race so hard to run,

Then I say to my soul, take courage,
the Lord will make a way somehow.

It is because of that kind of first-hand
determination that Valerie Martin-
Stewart has spoken. This volume is but an
invitation to trust in God sincerely,
believe in His power deeply, read His
Word faithfully, pray to Him believing, - -
and be healed.

The Rev. Henry Bradford, Jr., M.Div.,
Ed.D

University Chaplain (Retired) and a
Pastor Emeritus

GREETINGS

I was born in Water Valley, Mississippi. I lived with my Mom and Dad from an infant to three years old. However, at the age of four years old, they took me to live with my maternal grandmother, Annie B. Hervey. My Mom's baby sister, Aunt Janice, and her two children, Vanessa and George, lived in the house also. Later, their sister Ellen came along. Understand that I never mind visiting grandma's house on the weekends nor playing with my first cousins, but to have to live there for a year while I knew I had older brothers and sisters made me sad.

I wanted to live with my Mom and my brothers and sisters. I desired desperately to go home and play with my sister Beverly who was two years older than I was. Mama would come on weekends and take me home with her, but soon came Sunday evening, I found myself being taken *back* to grandma's house against my will. I wanted Beverly to stay with me at grandma's house since I realized I had to stay, but she didn't. This was the beginning of me feeling rejected and not wanted. Below, you are about to read the Divine Revelation just as it was given to me on that day in 2003. I've been instructed by God to not alter any of the words (except for the removal of some names), so that you will truly grasp and feel this deep revelation and know that it is from God and not from me.

THE MORNING IN OCTOBER

I had asked a close friend this day to go to lunch after church and she couldn't. Rejection overwhelmed me once again as it had many times before. There were things I desired to share with her; however, I found myself allowing her "no" response to take me deeper into that pit of rejection - a very dark and gloomy place. I was hurting and feeling really bad but I didn't fully understand why. (Later in this book, you will read the divine revelation God gave to me concerning the relationship with this friend) As I left church and drove home to pack for my trip to Nashville, I found myself crying but as soon as someone looked into my car, I'd dry my face quickly not wanting them to see me cry. However, when I walked into my house, I broke. I begin to cry and weep uncontrollably it seemed. The rejection I felt was beyond my explanation and your imagination. Then I heard the Holy Ghost immediately ask me if I knew why I was crying and why I couldn't cry in public. Well...I knew I was feeling rejected is "why" I was crying but later I learned (through divine revelation), that it wasn't the adult Val that was feeling rejected but the "little girl" who was living on the inside.

Now, as to why I didn't want anyone to see me cry in public, I didn't know...except I've felt this way all of my life. I never imagined that it was a stronghold. God then began to minister unto me about the "little girl" who had felt so much rejection daily as a youngster that now had hardened herself. This was very painful to me and I wondered why was God intentionally trying to hurt me. I wondered why He was talking to me about a "little girl" inside of me now, after all of these years. My thoughts were, "I'm grown now." Yet little did I know that there truly was a "little girl" way down on the inside that was about to be exposed this day like never before. It was indeed devastating unto me. *This was only the beginning of what was about to be revealed*!!! Little did I know that when God brought these painful memories into my mind that He was about to perform *supernatural* healing in my life! We must know that God doesn't do *something* for *nothing*. He's not out to reveal and expose our hurt and pain only to leave us in that condition. No! He reveals and allows us to feel so we will *know* once we are healed.

THE DRIVE TO NASHVILLE

As I traveled to Nashville that beautiful sunny day in 2003, I had called each of my siblings one by one. I didn't talk long. Understand that I've never called them frequently and *never* had I called all six of them on the same day. Unknown to me, God later revealed to me, once I reached Nashville, that I was saying my goodbyes to each of them. You see, the spirit of depression and suicide were taking me over. I was very depressed and feeling rejected mainly because I knew God had deposited a whole lot in me from a young girl and now He was working mightily in my life! However, of all the sermons and teaching outlines that were being given to me in my quiet time, it seems the opportunities to preach and teach them weren't coming fast enough. In spite of all of my travels both national and international, awards and accolades, I found myself very, very unfulfilled with life. Have you ever visited there? It's a lonely and dangerous place to go.

Yet, I later discovered that as I began to step out of fear and do what God had put in me to do…it was there I realized that my desires to minister God's word were directly connected to someone's need. I simply had to align and position myself with His will. I had to *get up* and be willing to *go out* and minister to the hurting and broken everywhere and not stay within the four corners of *any* church. I had to come w-a-y out of my comfort zone. Are you comfortable right now with your position in life and your service to God? If so, you need to move and move today! God is not calling us to comfort but to commitment. As I began to go out, doors begin to swing wide open for me to deliver each and every sermon and teaching outline. Wow! God is awesome!!

While still driving to Nashville, I heard someone telling me about all the successes I had achieved in life and all the good things I had accomplished. I began to reminisce as I heard each and every word and reflected on the people, places and events that had taken place in my life up to that point. But then, without warning, without notice, the voice told me that I was still lonely, depressed, and had no one to share all of my successes with. He reminded me that the marriage I had so desired had failed. He tried to sum up my life as nothingness, and wanted me to be convinced of this due to one of the major failures in my life.

At this awe-struck moment, I heard him telling me to look into my rear view mirror and that an eighteen-wheeler was coming. I looked in the mirror and sure enough, this eighteen-wheeler was coming on my left side. I was shocked! I knew immediately that this was the devil. And though I was feeling very low, I was not ready to give up! He told me to turn left at the precise time when he would instruct me to do so and that I would die instantly!!! He told me all of my pain, hurt, and feelings of rejection would be gone! He told me if I turned when he told me to, I wouldn't have to worry about *not* dying and being a paraplegic all of my life. As you see, I didn't listen to the voice, and I made it to Nashville where God *immediately* gave me this second book. He told me to get a pen and paper and to start writing what I heard.

The devil was telling me that yes, I've succeeded in this and accomplished that, but he reminded me of the areas that I had failed in life. He magnified my failures this day. Instead of me thanking God for all the good things and good people He had brought my way, I found myself drowning deeply in my failures and disappointments in life. Satan did this same thing to Eve in the garden. He caused her to focus on the *one* tree that was forbidden instead of her enjoying the many trees and fruit that she had been given free access to. All because she lost her focus, she found herself in opposition with the Almighty. I pray that you will not allow him to torment you in your mind with your past failures another day! To every reader, please take great notice to the fact that moments before this DIVINE REVELATION was revealed unto me, the enemy was tempting me to end my life by pulling out in front of that eighteen-wheeler!!! They say, "There is a thin line between love and hate" but it appears to be even a thinner line between good and evil, right versus wrong, hell versus heaven. Are you at the end of your rope? Are you feeling down, disappointed, and disgusted with life? Hold On! You too are about to experience a divine breakthrough!!!!

ONCE IN NASHVILLE, THE DIVINE REVELATION

I really don't know where to start. And honestly, I don't know who is talking, writing, or putting thoughts together in me. Is it the "little girl" talking or is it "Val," the one I've created to face the world? The one who has known a lot, and actually too much pain. And because of the pain I experienced early on, I put a shield purposely around my heart. I have trained myself to perform at a high level. I've put extreme pressure on myself to excel in all that I've put my hands to. But even in this, I always looked to others, anybody, in my circle, for approval to validate me. Validate my looks, my performance, my walk and talk. And if just one had something negative to say, I'd go back, examine myself and put even greater and stricter demands on myself to get approval from all. What I've discovered in this is that people are harsh, mean and some very cold-blooded creatures.

In the Book of Jeremiah 17: 9, it tells us that "the heart is deceitful above all things and desperately wicked; who can know it?" So, time, hurts, pain, wounds, and God have taught me to try to find that peaceful place, that rest in God and God alone. I've lost many friends and associates by doing so. Some were only friendly enemies. But me? I'm growing in peace day by day. I realize that this peaceful place is not a " physical place," but it's something spiritual and beneficial in and along the journey.

I'm thirty-seven years old now. And it's taken this long to find out why I have great problems when it comes to expressing myself. I've always hated for anyone to see me cry. I learned to toughen myself at all cost. It has taken God to reveal to me the rejection I experienced at four years old by my mother has damaged my emotions in ways I cannot tell on this paper. I'm beginning to cry now, because whenever I think back on this time, the pain comes back, it returns, and it's as real and painful as it was back then.

No, no one is here with me, so I feel it's ok to cry now. But when I step outside (into the world), I feel I must be strong, hard core (my brother Bruce would say), tough, and pretend I'm all right. Does it hurt? Yes, very badly, but my Mom, who caused this pain and wounds, "unintentionally" I believe, is deceased. I can't tell her what she did to me. How she damaged me, day after day after day by showing up, bringing me ice cream, sometimes taking me for a ride, but then at the end of the day, she'd leave me again. Same story. You want to hear it? It simply went like this.

"Mama, can I go? Can I go home with you today? Please? Please Mama?" Mama would tell me okay and she'd tell my cousin Vanessa to take me to the back to get my coat. Yes, you know what happened next, right? When I returned to the front of the house all excited with my little red coat on, Mama was gone. And I asked myself "why?" Why does she keep teasing me? Why does she keep coming by to see me everyday, only to leave me?" More than that, I've wondered all of my life <u>what's wrong with me</u>? Why wasn't I good enough to take home by my Mom? Why couldn't I live with my other brothers and sisters? Was I ugly, did I stink; did I have some physical handicaps that embarrassed my Mama? What? What was it?

So, night after night, I'd crawl behind my grandmother and just cry and cry until I'd cry myself to sleep. Just like I felt my Mama really must have disliked me to constantly come by but leave me, I tried to dislike her. I had "internally" built a shelter for my heart. After crying all of those nights, I was determined deep down on the inside that no one would ever, ever, make nor see me cry again. So, I suppressed my tears for years until it became impossible for me to cry publicly, no matter how much I desired to. Why? Because I felt if my own Mama didn't care, the world surely wouldn't. I've trained myself to be tough, funny, comical, self-driven and motivated; yet I still looked for love and approval and too many times, in all the wrong faces, spaces and places.

I've obtained a Computer Science degree, Electrical Engineering degree, and a Master's in Biblical Studies. I've played professional basketball and was blessed to travel internationally and lived in Lima, Peru, all cities in Australia as I worked as a Computer Analyst for the Australian Government, and traveled to Milan, Bari, and Rome, Italy on a tour. I've met a lot of people; talked to them as they shared their story and I shared my story (but not this story).

People from all walks of life and different countries have called me smart, very intelligent, very articulate, soft-spoken, and quiet to name a few. But let the truth be known, I'm not that smart. Honestly, because every degree I received except my

Master's, I had to put extreme pressure and demands on myself. I had to gain my focus in a way that pained me to do so. I obtained a personal tutor to get me through engineering. His name was Frank from Africa. I seriously told him that he should be the one getting my degree on the day of graduation. So, you see, I've had to go to some extreme measures to make average grades (Cs) not A(s) and B(s) in my Computer Science and Engineering programs.

I've always been slow. People have always laughed and made fun of my speech saying how slowly I talked and walked. This damaged me also. So, I learned silence and set myself to be quiet in any group setting so I wouldn't be made fun of. Understand now, not just as a little girl, but as a grown person also. I sit, listen intently, and process all that is being said. I'm a hard and deep thinker – sometimes I hate the fact that I am. Don't get me wrong – I always have something to share, things I want to project or inject into people's minds for consideration. But fear of being laughed at causes me to keep silent. I don't want any pity, never did as a little girl, and definitely not now. But I will tell you this. I was run over by a car when I was four years old. I was knocked unconscious. All I remember is my Mama jumping and running from the car to hurry into a store (I guess to pay a bill) and she told my first cousin Steve to get my hand and help me across the street. I didn't wait on Steve. I took off running after Mama. Why, you make ask? Well…I thought Mama was leaving me again like all the times she'd left me at grandmother's house. I was determined to stay with her this day while she was in sight. She never knew I was running behind her and I never made it across the street to reach my Mama. A car hit me, causing the bumper to hit me on the side of my head. I woke up in the hospital with many people standing around me. I recall the doctor shaving hair off the side of my head. Why, I don't know. I remember him telling Mama that I would need glasses one day because of this (I wear contacts now). Don't ask me how I know, but I believe this car accident caused things within my mind to slow up. My thoughts are slow and therefore they are reflected in my speech, which has been slow for years. I'm a little faster at them all than I used to be. That's that.

I started writing spiritual poetry when I was in the 6th grade, about twelve years old. It was a way of expressing myself when I felt I couldn't talk to others without them making fun. I could write and not be worried about anyone making fun of that. Even if they read my writings, they wouldn't know how long it took me to gather my thoughts. Whether my thoughts were slow or fast, they wouldn't know. They would merely read words on a piece of paper. This was healing for me as well as safe, for my speech wasn't needed to write. God later revealed to me that I had a "gift" of writing. I was totally shocked, because even though I didn't know the gifts of God, I never imagined writing could be one. I accepted that fact and continued to write off and on as I chose. God later spoke to me again and told me that it's a gift. In other words, not self-given or man-given, but given strictly by Him. Therefore, He was stressing the fact to me that I must write when He (the Holy Spirit) moves on me to write, not just when I felt like it. This was shocking news also, but have I always obeyed? Well…no. I've been slack, very slack at times.

God has always spoken to me in dreams and visions from as early as 7th grade that I can remember. I used to have visions about my family, friends, and almost anyone. I still do. The scary thing was, the visions would come to pass immediately, like the same day or the next day. As I slowly began to tell people what I had seen by way of dreams and visions, they would call me crazy and tell me not to be dreaming about them. Well…I couldn't control this. I never asked to dream or see anything about anybody. I didn't know such thing was even possible. Since then, I've accepted this gift as some have called it prophecy. I don't clearly know. I just accept it and the things I'm shown. I'm more at ease now with telling people what I see. I used to fear their rejection of me and my dreams and visions. But I don't fear that anymore. Do I still get rejected? Of course, all the time, but it doesn't bother me anymore. I want to please God. I have a heart and made up mind to do so. I know that it's better to suffer for doing good rather than to suffer for doing evil. This is Scripture.

God was calling me to preach around the 11th grade (1983). This totally put fear, doubt, and uncertainty in me! How? How could He when we were taught that God doesn't call women to preach, only to be missionaries? I had accepted that as a fact and embraced it as "doctrine." Yet the "call" got stronger and it grew bigger in me day by day. I was scared! I told no one! I knew all of these thoughts about me preaching were insane! So, I tried day by day to block them out. I noticed the more I read my Bible the stronger and more intense the thoughts would be about preaching. So, I chose to stop reading my Bible for periods of time. But then mothers in the church started having visions about me. They would tell Mama. Mama would approach me in an angry and bitter way, wanting to know what was going on. I couldn't tell her. I didn't know. Then my step-father told her I was different from all her other children and that one day I would change from Baptist to something else (another denomination) for he told her I love to express myself. Once again, Mama approached me demanding a response and telling me all at the same time that I was Baptist and always would be. I wondered in

*my head, "why all the fuss" because I
didn't know of any other denomination but
Methodist. (Smile) And they seemed like
Baptist to me. So, I didn't have a clue
about what my stepfather saw and why he
told her those things. So, I accepted what
my Mama told me outwardly, but
"inwardly," deep on the inside,
"something" told me I must obey God
rather than my Mama. In the Book of
Psalms 118: 8 says, "It is better to trust in
Lord than to put confidence in man." And
the main scripture that would burn in me
since I was in the 7th grade was Matthew
10:28 which says, "And fear not them
which kill the body, but are not able to kill
the soul; but rather fear him which is able
to destroy both soul and body in hell." I
fear God, always have and always will.*

*As the mothers continued to have visions of
me, my Mama continued to demand
answers from me. By the way, their visions
were of me wearing a long white robe,
walking down our church aisle, leading
masses of people. They saw blacks, whites,
and many other races of people both young
and old following me. One mother dreamed
I was in a huge mall parking lot and that*

no cars were there. I was standing on a few steps with thousands of people gathered around me. She told Mama as these thousands of people gathered, that I stood before them with an opened Bible in my hand. You may be wondering how I remember these dreams so well even though I was only in the 6th and 7th grade, right? Well…I eventually started having the exact same dreams. It's scary, I know! How do you think I felt all of these years, especially as a young teen? Trying to obey my parents and not defy God was a constant battle within. I don't know how soon it was, but I eventually confronted my Mama and told her I must obey God rather than her. I was respectful, but I recall she only stared at me, not saying anything.

Well…I've shared this to say and come to this conclusion. God had our lives mapped out and planned from the very beginning. He will show others and us things about ourselves. We are the ones who'll determine whether we'll ever walk in His already mapped out plan or choose our own way. I've chosen my own way many, many times in many of things, but I'm back here now…seeking God's divine plan.

I've come to the conclusion about my rejection that I experienced as early as four years old these facts: when I consider what happened to me then and when I consider all that I've been through up to now, that God knew/knows everything about me. He knows about my shortcomings, hurts, wounds, insecurities and so on. Even though man has rejected me and made fun of me, laughed at me, and about me, God still, in spite of all of their jokes, has chosen to call me. He has entrusted me enough to show me dreams and visions; showed others dreams and visions about me so that I wouldn't think I'm crazy. He's done all of this to say to me that "Val, I love you and in spite of what you've been through, in spite of what the world thinks of you, I want to use you."

God knew about the tears I cried over and over, night after night as I lay behind my grandmother. He knows how I now have trouble showing my emotions. Be it that I'm happy, sad, angry, or glad. I've trained myself to suppress them all. That old saying, "don't let them see you sweat" is true. But mine was "don't let them see you cry." But I desire to cry openly now. I want to tell people I'm mad when they've made me mad. I want to be able to shout, scream, run, and jump whether happy or sad when I'm feeling this way. I simply want to believe somehow that my gifting to preach the Gospel of Jesus, my gifting of writing, my gifting to heal with the laying on of my hands are all supposed to come together and tie in with my feelings and living with rejection all of my life. I believe God has a plan to use all of this to heal me and yet set many others free that I believe are living with this same problem. Glory be to God!

It's painful to expose oneself openly to everyone. To remove the cover, shell, wall of protection from my heart that I have shielded myself with for thirty-two years. It's not easy. But the thought of one person sharing and exposing herself so that thousands may be set free, I'd say, I'm willing. I want to help heal all of those who like myself have learned to live with depression, feelings of rejections, the spirit of suicide, and not ever feeling good enough. I choose to be free!!! I choose to live life and live it in an abundant manner! No more hiding Val! No more being afraid. No more fear of being rejected or accepted.

No more! I choose to love! I choose to uncover and expose my wounds so that many can get help, get healing, and get their souls back. In the Book of Isaiah 53: 5 says, "But He was wounded for our transgressions, He was bruised for our iniquities; the chastisement of our peace was upon Him and with His stripes we are healed." It's amazing how one man's suffering brought and can bring healing to millions! But remember, He's not just any man; He's God Man. His name is Jesus! Awesome Counselor and Ruler is He!

Lately, I've come to the conclusion that I really don't know who I am. I'm yet learning about Val. What I like and dislike. Why, you may ask? Because majority of my life has been spent trying to be what others wanted me to be. I've lived with a stone wall around my heart, and not allowing people to get close to me and share some of my feelings. Overall, I've kept people away from touching my emotions. I internalized all of my feelings of hatred, anger, depression, the need for approval from teachers, coaches, friends, boyfriends, and even this elder who became a very close friend. You see, this friend and I began to talk at the time my Mama was very ill with terminal cancer. Soon after my Mama died, I drew very close to this friend. Actually, when I look back at it, I really had begun to draw close to her while my Mama yet lived. Because each visit to my Mama's bedside made me realize the truth, that she was not getting up again from her illness.

I initially drew close to her because of her personality and loving nature. She's very loving, caring and gentle when it comes to people. She's sweet like you wouldn't believe. She has something so awesome about her that works like a magnet. It draws you to her if you ever talk to her and get in her presence. I believe it's the very love of God that she possesses so strongly. I've never known or met anyone in all of my travel that drew me like she has. And it's not just me. It's everyone who comes into contact with her. I've witnessed other leaders and professors speak about her in a way that even they found hard to explain. They tried to formulate into words a true description of who she is and the kind of person she is. They all would conclude that there is "something" about her that they too have never seen nor felt in anyone else.

To truly witness some of what I'm trying to explain, just come to one of her services on any Sunday and look at the long lines of people that wait to hug her, talk to her, and just have her to talk back. It's a symbol of how it must have been when Jesus walked the dusty roads of Galilee. Secondly, I drew close to her because I knew I was being called to preach and I knew she could relate with this calling. I knew without any doubt she could give me instructions and guidance. She did, as she was very, very helpful and inspiring. A lot of what she told me I didn't want to hear nor embrace because accepting a call to preach was nothing I wanted to do.

Even though she and I started talking in 1991, I still didn't acknowledge my call publicly until June 1997. Thirdly, I drew close to her because I needed and wanted a Mom in my life and she just seemed to care in such a way that she easily became Mama's replacement for me without my awareness. *And the Holy Spirit gave me a divine revelation about this relationship with her this same day also. He revealed unto me that whenever I asked her to do this or go here or there with me and she* *didn't, I got my feelings hurt, feeling rejected again. I fell right back into that pit of rejection from when I was four years old. This is when the "little girl" rose up in me and I NEVER KNEW IT. I would lash out at her a lot of times when it was really Mama who I was "internally" speaking to. No matter what the question was that I'd ask my friend, if her answer was no, I (the "little girl" inside) heard "no, you can't go home with me today either." The words I <u>never</u> heard from my Mama but was shown by her actions. Actions truly do speak louder than words. Every time my Mama told Vanessa to take me to the back to get my coat, when I returned and found her gone, her actions yelled, screamed and vibrated in my ears and mind a resounding, "NO!" So, you see if I asked this friend to go to lunch with me and she answered yes, I was fine. But if she told me no, I wouldn't hear, "No Val, I can't go to lunch with you today." The "little girl" would rise inside of me and hear, "No, you can't go home with me today." I know this sounds strange; well it did to me when it was revealed to me, but it makes a lot of sense to me and brings clarity to so much of my pain and actions.*

To me, nothing is better in life than to find out whom you are and what's really to you; why you behave as you do, say and do the things you do. I believe many people have lived and will continue to live on this earth (long lives no doubt) and die, having never discovered who they really were...all because they lived a life trying to "be like" someone else. If each of us could ever get to the bottom of who we really are, then it's at that place and point in our lives, I believe we would experience great healing. Not only do I believe we would experience healing, but we would turn the world upside down with our individuality, uniqueness and power in God. Too many people have grown up physically, but still a "little child" mentally and emotionally. Scarred and wounded by childhood happenings. For some it was molestation and rape by family members and for others it was abuse both sexually and physically. Many have been told all of their lives that they would NEVER be anything in life or they'd be just like their no-good daddies. Can't you hear it...one curse spoken after another? Listen to this viscous, repetitive cycle...an evil that we must break. Many *generational curses must be broken over thousands of families. It's then and only then will families come together and find their rightful places in the Kingdom <u>right here on earth</u>.*

So, understand that I tried to set myself against my Mama at four years old internally. Oh, I loved her, but I tried to condition myself, my heart and mind to dislike her, but I couldn't. Really, because I thought she disliked me for not taking me home with her. I wanted to not be moved by her disappointing me; her making me cry. Because of all of those tears, I was determined to never cry again. And this is what I told myself for nearly thirty-two years.

Lastly, after I had written approximately twelve pages on legal paper, the Holy Ghost told me to stop writing and to call this elder, close friend and mentor of mine to ask her if I could read the pages to her. He told me that she would understand the things that I had written under the unction of the Holy Ghost and be able to shed more light on them. I called her and she told me I could share what I wanted to share. After

I finished reading the pages of revelation, very earth-moving and nerve-shaking to me, to my surprise, my friend revealed to me that she had <u>met</u> the "little girl" and on several occasions had spoken unto her!!! You must understand that this was very shocking and scary for me. I wanted to know more on one hand about her dealings with the "little girl" but on the other hand I feared what might be revealed unto me. My thoughts were racing and my adrenaline had reached its maximum! How could this close friend know and be aware of the "little girl" for years, when I was JUST coming into the revelation knowledge about the "little girl" for the first time on this day? Shouldn't I know myself? I fearfully wondered how many others had met the "little girl" and if they recognized her? I asked my friend and mentor questions about the "little girl" in fear, but I wanted to <u>completely</u> get free of my past! God had truly opened me up and exposed me to myself and that was very mind-boggling. I felt total embarrassment on one hand, but divine healing taking place on the other hand. On this day, SUPERNATURAL healing began in my life from the spirit of rejection and all of *her relatives. Some of those are: feelings of abandonment, depression, suicidal thoughts, addictions, self-hatred, low self-esteem, and feeling inadequate just to name a few. So ends the "Divine Revelation."*

"THE PHASES OF REJECTION"

SELF-HATRED

At the age of four years old, I began to totally hate myself and everything about myself. Somehow, I couldn't understand why my Mom kept all of my other brothers and sisters at her house, but not me. What was wrong with me? This was a question I thought about over and over and over again. Self-hatred is a very strong emotion and one that is hard to break free of without the intervention of God.

I hated the way I talked because everyone always made fun of that. So, I learned silence. And silence became a security blanket for me. Oh, I always had things to say, expressions I wanted to share from a little girl to now. But fear of being laughed at caused me to keep quiet. Even now, I still struggle with expressing myself in a group setting, no matter how small or large the group.

I learned to love being in the background trying to hide from everyone. Not wanting to be seen or heard. We need to understand that self-hatred will cause us to inflict pain upon ourselves. How, you may ask? I've discovered that when we really don't know who we are, we allow others to define us by their inferiorities and their insecurities. We soon find ourselves like the Prodigal Son in the fifteenth chapter of Luke's gospel. We end up taking our "prized possessions" and go live the fast life only to find ourselves in the "hog pens" of life. What are some of those "hog pens?" I'm glad you asked. Just to name a few of these "hog pens" are: elicit sexual relationships, overeating, drug and alcohol addictions, lying, gossiping, overspending, judging others, and the list goes on. Living in any of these "hog pens" of life will cause our views to become distorted and *muddy* and we become unable to rightly see the value and good in others, let alone ourselves. Hog pens cause our feet to become "stuck" in the mud. (The mud of disappointments, disillusions, and setbacks) The very wings (eagle-like) according to Isaiah 40: 31 that God has given us to soar to new heights, get wet and weighted down with mud and disables us to fly. And because we are stuck, muddy, and weighted down, our view of others are "dirty." How do we get out of and overcome the "hog pens" of life? We get out and overcome them by first repenting unto God and asking Him for restoration. Then we must return *home* to all of those whom we've mistreated and sinned against and repent. Then and only then can we start seeing ourselves for who we really are in Christ Jesus. Self-hatred is ugly, depressing and a destroyer of our spirits. It is through Jesus and His blood alone do we escape the "hog pens."

Learn to love yourself. This includes how you walk, talk, look, accepting the color of your skin, your race whether black, white, Mexican, Asian, Hispanic, Latino or any other. It's who you are. It's who God made you to be. Know that you can never truly love yourself and others until you allow God to love you with His unconditional love. In Matthew 22:37, 39, Jesus tells us what the greatest commandments are: "Thy shalt love the Lord thy God with all thy heart, and with all thy soul and with all thy mind. And the second is like unto it, thy shalt love thy neighbor as thyself." I discovered that many people, including myself, allow others to mistreat and mishandle us when we don't truly love ourselves. We accept their ideas and ways to be the right way over our very own. Due to the lack of self-love, we go through extreme measures trying to "fit in" and belong.

Self-hatred is a very real and ugly thing. But the opposite of it is love. Embrace God, Jesus, and our Helper, our Friend, our Comforter, our Teacher and Guide, the Holy Spirit. Then embrace and love yourself. Love the fact that you are different. Love the fact that you are unique and you "don't fit in," because neither did Jesus. Yet it never faced Him.

Simply because He was confident in whom He was and is. Today, right now, stop living in the "hog pens" of life. Get up! Shake off the mud, go and wash yourself and *fly* back home!

LOW SELF-ESTEEM

As a result of my feelings of rejection all of my life, I've battled very, very low self-esteem more than half of my life. Being a starter of my junior high, high school, collegiate and professional basketball teams really launched me in front of people much earlier than I ever wanted or desired. I was moved to the high school team to be the starting point guard during my 9th - grade year. This was very challenging for me because I didn't want to be moved. I wanted to stay on my 9th grade team and play ball with my cousins and friends. Yet we went to state my 10th grade year and playing in Jackson, Mississippi, in the Coliseum was very overwhelming for me. We played before our largest crowd ever. Feelings of joy gripped me on the one hand, to have made it so far in our playoffs. Yet feelings of devastation and fear had a hold of me on the other because so many eyes would be watching my teammates and me.

Anyone who has dealt with or knows a person with low self-esteem knows that she/he does not want to be seen nor heard if all possible. So, many have mistaken my involvement with sports and civic clubs as a definite cue that I was outgoing, fun-filled, and witty. No, I was far from them all. I just happened to be good in basketball because I played so much as a little girl with my sisters, brothers, and cousins at home every day. Later, I realized that basketball was a "form of release" for me just like writing. It gave me satisfaction and brought me fulfillment to interact with other young ladies. I often made them laugh, telling jokes, and being real silly. However, at the same time, I was always in deep thought and meditation in almost every setting where I found myself.

My feelings of low self-esteem caused me to walk with my head down, and not look people in the eye when I talked to them or they talked to me and I would just sit and wander many times in thought. I've always heard people say that if a person can't look you in the eye when talking, then they are lying. I always knew that this was not the truth. Many times I didn't and wouldn't look others in the eye due to my feelings of unworthiness, but I *was* telling the truth. And often, I saw others look people dead in the eye and lie about things I knew to be the truth.

Living with low self-esteem caused me to always believe everyone else was smarter than I, was more beautiful than I was, knew so much more than I, and could do *it* (which included everything) better than I could. I have *always* felt inferior, not just in my white racial contacts, but to everyone. I became very, very introverted. I always found myself in very deep thought about almost everything, but mainly about people and about life. I realized that in my silence and by observing others, I could learn a lot, and so much about others without ever having a direct conversation with them. And it's not always what they say that you will see, but all the things they *never* said, which is the non-verbal communication. It's true that only 10% of communication is verbal while 90% of communication is through body language. I had believed it to be the other way around for years because of all the "talk" that people do and say; always having an opinion about everything and trying to project this thought or another into the head of the listener or observer.

Living with low self-esteem also caused me to allow others, especially boyfriends, to take advantage of me. Many times I accepted their lies, their schemes and game playing just to feel loved and accepted. Many times while knowing and seeing the truth, I pretended not to see or know so that I wouldn't be alone. While they and many others have always told me how pretty I was, I never saw myself as pretty nor felt pretty. It's not what's on the outside that makes us pretty, but how we feel on the inside. Truly, I have talked to so many gorgeous, beautiful, and talented women who were all made up on the outside and had it "going on" in their dress, hair, makeup, and shoes but expressed deep hurt, pain, guilt and shame on the inside. I've never wanted to be a fake. I've never wanted to appear to be one thing and really feel another. I don't like phony people; neither do I like to be entertained by them. To be real and keep it real is how I've tried to live my life. So, when anyone saw me looking sad, feeling low, depressed and *out of it,* I was. Low self-esteem will cause an individual to withdraw, isolate, deflate, and suppress all the pain being felt on the inside.

DEPRESSION

Wow! This very subject is one that I'm well acquainted with. I've felt it, carried it, slept with it, functioned through it, and made it my bed covers in the night. I've been very, very depressed most of my life...all of my life, except for the last couple of years. I have laughed with it, smiled through it, and even gave birth to it. I've never really functioned without it. I simply thought this is the way life is supposed to be. I concluded that feeling the way I did and have for most of my life was *normal.* I didn't know life could be sweeter and that I could feel so much better until the Holy Spirit revealed unto me that I was carrying a "spirit of depression" and that I needed to be delivered from it. All I knew was that I didn't feel happy *most* of the time. Sure, there were many times I laughed and made others laugh, but deep within, there was no real joy. My happy spurts came and went and they "went" more than they came.

Feelings of depression caused me to think about suicide most of my life. This started around twelve years old. I recall writing out my obituary in junior high school because I always felt I would die young. I've always been afraid to kill myself for fear of burning in hell eternally, but it didn't keep me from thinking about it often.

The really sad part about depression is that I like many others, remained very functional and performed well in school (graduating with honors in high school) and became a basketball standout among my high school, collegiate, and international teams. I received many awards in sports and on my jobs with the Australian government and for the U.S. Army. I was a part of many clubs and organizations and was even president of the Fellowship of Christian Athletes. Yet in all of this, I felt heavy, burdened, and weighted down by depression. I smiled through *it* for the cameras, interviewed with *it* for the news reporters, and hid *it* while trying to work.

Depression caused me to start drinking in college, trying to kill and numb the pain. I never liked the taste of alcohol in any form, so I drank it fast to avoid the taste while hoping I could relax and be free of my pain. (If only temporary) It never worked so I soon stopped that madness. Depression is a silent killer, because some of its relatives are stress, high blood pressure, obesity, headaches, strokes, heart attacks, and tension.

SUICIDAL THOUGHTS

Often thoughts of being tired of living and feeling unfulfilled with life bombarded my mind. I vividly recall in Jr. High that I wrote my obituary out because I always felt that I would die at a young age. I never had the nerves to take my own life, because we were taught that if one did, she or he was going straight to hell. But the thoughts wouldn't leave me alone.

Sure, there were times I was happy and displayed it very well and usually made others laugh too. However, when I would get by myself, I would find myself deep in thought of how my family would get along without me. Deep inside, I've always felt there was more to life than what I was experiencing. I desired more, and never felt totally fulfilled in the many friendships, organizations, and activities that I found myself involved in. Playing sports and writing relieved a lot of the tension for me.

Another divine revelation or vision was given to me my senior year in high school which also made me believe I wouldn't live long and that was okay with me. During my senior year, I recall that every time we played our arch rivalry Oxford High, that it would rain. My friend Shannon Rowland and I took notice to that. We had many spiritual talks. One night in November 1983 at Oxford High gymnasium, as we were dressing after our game was over, Shannon gave me one of her tennis shoes asking me to hold it until after Thanksgiving break. I told her it didn't make sense to take just one shoe, so give me both of them. She assured me that one shoe fitted perfectly in her bag, but both would not and she just needed me to take one shoe home with me. We went back and forth until I finally realized she wasn't going to give me the other shoe so I just stuffed her one shoe in my bag. As we sat in the gym watching the boys play and all of the girls were talking and laughing, I began to feel "strange."

It was a funny feeling but I didn't have a clue as to what it was so I dismissed it. At half-time of the boys game, Shannon and her parents got up to leave for home and that's when the "feeling" came back again but stronger and I heard these words – "Say goodbye to Shannon because one of you all will not live past Thanksgiving (if I recall correctly)." I dismissed the thought and kept trying to laugh and talk with my teammates. However, as Shannon and her parents were still walking towards the door to exit the gym, the voice came again. Only except it was stronger and with more force the next few times. So I immediately jumped to my feet, feeling r-e-a-l strange and I took my umbrella and rushed to the gymnasium door as Shannon was about to walk out and I touched her with it right in the bend of her leg. She turned around and as I'm sure I was looking stupid, I told her goodbye. I vividly recall that Shannon never said a word but gave me a huge smile and walked out. I can still see her smile today. I went back to my seat believing for sure now that it was I. I knew for sure that I would be the one to pass and never see Shannon or anyone else again. But honestly, I didn't feel sad or depressed about it.

Amazingly, my sister Joyce received a phone call the very next night (or two) that Shannon and her sister Robin had been in a terrible car accident where Robin was killed instantly and Shannon was hanging on to dear life. Whoever was on the line told my sister that Shannon wanted to see all of her basketball teammates, but especially me, stating that she had lost one of her legs in the wreck. (I wonder to this day did I have the same shoe to the foot she lost) Instantly, I was reminded of the "inner voice" I had heard the night before and I knew at this awe-struck moment that it was Shannon. I sadly told Joyce that we had no time to get to the hospital, as I knew for sure I had truly seen her for the last time at the game just as I had heard. Yet my sister told me to stop being weird and just come on and let's go. Within moments of the first phone call, a second one came in and we found out that Shannon had passed away also with her sister.

I was led to write a poem to Mrs. Rowland in honor of Shannon and Robin called "Death is only the Beginning" which is published in my first book "Out of Pain Came Poetry." I grieved on the inside very deeply for the loss of my friend Shannon and for Mr. and Mrs. Rowland for the loss of not one but two of their daughters. However, part of me envied Shannon for "having life made now." I knew Shannon was born again from our many discussions about Christ, so I knew she was better off than me. Some parts of me became angry with God for taking her and not me. This is just how bad the spirit of suicide weighed me down. Darkness has always seemed to follow me. I needed deliverance badly from this spirit, but it never came. Yet many friends and strangers have always told me they saw a "glow" around me.

PERFECTIONIST

Lastly, I became a perfectionist, wanting everything to be as clean and as neat as possible. This included from cleaning to getting things perfectly right whether at home, work, or in relationships. From playing sports, I learned to be very competitive on and off the court. And I believe from competing in sports all of those years came my need for approval and being a perfectionist. I've never like anyone giving me compliments, because I always felt so undeserving. As Joyce listened to others give me compliments and watched my head drop, she would tell me, "Val, tell them thank you. You don't even know how to take a compliment." And the truth is, she was right.

However, I wanted to perform well in the classroom and on the court to show people I was athletic and smart and give them reasons to like me. Even today, I'm still a perfectionist when it comes to so many things. My daughter Paris probably suffers the worse from my need for everything being in order. If we are cleaning the house, I can't stand for anything to be left on the counter or floor and yes, I'm talking about a piece of hair or a fuzz ball from the carpet or what have you.

Because I have lived my life looking for approval from others, I have never really lived my own life. I tell people now that I really don't know who I am anymore, because all of my life has been spent trying to please others from my mother, siblings, coaches, teachers, boyfriends, and the list goes on. Now that I've been delivered from this spirit of rejection, I don't feel the need for anyone to validate me anymore to say, "Yes Val, that's right, you're doing a great job." My biggest challenge now is trying to find out who I really am, get in touch with my inner, positive feelings and follow my passions. It seems God is taking me really fast now that I'm tuning in to Him and wanting His validation and not others.

For sure, these are not all the characteristics of rejection, but these are some that have haunted me for most of my young and adult life.

Rejection Was Really My Protection

Though my Mom and I never sat down and talked about my feelings of rejection that I've carried all of my life, I have a better understanding of it all. I realize now, that what I perceived as rejection was really my Mama's protection of me. She was protecting me from having to stay home alone because her job started before my Head Start Bus would come and so did my sibling's bus come before mine. Had she not placed me with my grandmother, I would have not been able to attend Head Start. Mama was protecting me from being alone. The mere fact that she came by EVERY SINGLE DAY to visit me and bring me ice cream proved her love for me and her desire to be with me. However, she was just in a situation where I could not be with her and my siblings overnight. I know that she loved me with every part of her being. She, no doubt, saw the joy and delight in me and saw probably how my eyes lit up each time she brought me ice cream sandwiches everyday and so she never stopped by *without* one. (And I still LOVE ice cream sandwiches to this day) Thanks to Mama!

Just like my Mama was protecting me and not rejecting me, as I had believed – I thought about how Jesus must have felt on the Cross-when He was dying for your sins and mine. He cried out in pure anguish unto His Father, "My God, my God, why hast thou forsaken me?" (Matthew 27: 46b) Glory!!! Forsaken means to give up, renounce, and to leave altogether. Have you ever felt forsaken? There's hope and help available!

Jesus too, felt forsaken and rejected while He was dying for us on that bloody cross. He felt isolated and alone, as God did nothing. Yet, God was not rejecting Him but truly protecting Him. God had to close His eyes and turn His back on sin (Jesus was being made sin for us), as we know sin separates us from God. I believed had God turned and saw the pain, agony, and turmoil that His Son was travailing through He would have perhaps loosed Jesus from the nails and rescued Him. Then we would still be lost and bound for hell. But I thank God that He *rejected* Jesus long enough so that we might be *protected*. Jesus' suffering was not for Him at all but for us! Likewise, I believe many times we suffer not for ourselves but for someone else. Sure, some suffering is simply due to reaping what we've sown, but some suffering is truly for somebody else.

Yes, Jesus' rejection brought about our protection! He has protected us from hell's eternal fire, from being bound by the enemy, from living in fear, failure, shame and guilt, from every generational curse, from every work of the flesh and from being tormented by every demonic force and the devil. I'm now looking at the fact that in order for Jesus to have died for us to protect us from all of these things, He had to be *separated* from His Father for thirty-three years. Jesus' separation from God surely brought about some feelings of rejection.

Therefore, sometimes in life, in order to truly be protected, we may have to experience being rejected. Yes, I realize now that sometimes before we can be brought in, we must be put out; sometimes before we can fly high, we must travel low; sometimes before we can leap over mountains, we must tread through the valleys; sometimes before we can sit on the right hand of the Father, we must be spat on, beaten and nailed to a bloody Cross! Isaiah 53: 3 tells us, "He is despised and rejected of men; a man of sorrows and acquainted with grief and we hid as it were our faces from Him; He was despised and we esteemed Him not." Then verse 10a of this same chapter says, "Yet it pleased the Lord to bruise Him." Truly, Jesus experienced the *ultimate* rejection, but He had *our* protection in mind.

I can see clearly how what I perceived as *rejection* was really Mama's *protection* and now it has given me a new *direction*. I pray that you who read this have been enlightened about the subject of rejection and that healing has taken place in your own life. God desires for us to be healthy and whole Christians. When He began to reveal all of these painful things unto me, I was becoming angry with Him and asking Him why was He hurting me, so intentionally it seemed. I later realized that He was trying to make plain unto me that no matter how long we preach, teach, sing, dance, speak in tongues, shout, fall out, quote scriptures, and the like – until we allow His Word to saturate into those innermost places within us, those wounded and hurting places and heal us, we will never be able to be whole and walk in the true authority that has been given unto us.

For it's not in the preaching and teaching of the Word that heal us and make us whole, but it's in *living* the Word which we preach, teach, sing, dance, shout, and fall out about that makes us whole. The power of God is awesomely manifested in the "doing" of His Word. We must _apply_ the Word and not just read it, teach it, quote it, preach it, and sing it.
I'm very happy to announce that since the awesome revelation in 2003, I've been able to cry openly and publicly. (Before, I

had not cried openly for years) I've been able to express myself to others in love. I've been able to look people in the eye more and feel worthy. I've forgiven my Mother and released the pain of rejection from upon me even though she had no idea of the pain she caused. So, I say to each of you, release all of the people that have hurt you and allow God to open you up on the inside and perform spiritual surgery in all of those hurting and wounded places. More importantly, be determined to never intentionally reject others who come across your path. This includes your children, your spouse, love ones and strangers. "For some of us have entertained angels unaware."

CONCLUSION

Most black people say they feel hatred, rejection and mistreatment from the "white race." But my first-hand experience with rejection and what I felt to be mistreatment was felt from my encounter with my Mother leaving me at grandma's house. This caused me to develop a deep inferiority complex, because I felt unworthy as a child, which followed me into my adult life. However, I now realized the truth regarding the feelings of inferiority and I read it by an author unknown years ago. The words say: "No one can make you feel inferior *without* your consent." Oh, how true this statement is!

This tells me that we have control over our feelings and if we lose control, it's only because we released it to another. I believe that no matter how intelligent, outgoing, and bright others seem to excel in areas over us, we too have something *valuable* to offer. We must get in our place and realize that we have strong points as well as weak points. We must realize that we can't do everything well, but we can at least do some things well so, maximize those.

I did find the courage at seventeen years old, as I was a freshman in college, to write my Mother a letter asking her "why." I asked her why did I have to live with grandma. Mom did write me back and explained why. She told me she had to be at work before my Head Start bus would come and that my siblings' bus would come before mine. She told me I would have had to stay home alone and she wasn't about to do that. She did tell me that she never knew that I *didn't* know why I had to live there for a year. Her explanation helped bring clarity to my questions, but it didn't take away all the pain and feelings of rejection that I had felt and carried for all of those years. I had to look to God to bring about total and complete healing.

The Lord has been speaking to me in visions and dreams since I was twelve as I stated earlier. In the summer of 2006, I had a vision of me being at my grandmother's house which is in Water

Valley and that many family members and friends were there. I saw myself looking out the back door admiring all this beautiful fruit (grapes, oranges, and bananas), which were of a color purple, orange and yellow like I had never seen on this earth before. The amazing thing was that all of these fruits were on the same limb and I tried desperately to get everyone to come and see this awesome colored fruit. No one seemed interested and I heard a voice say to me, "They are not interested, but why don't *you* go and pick the fruit?" In this alone, John 15:16 comes to mind which states, "Ye have not chosen me, but I have chosen you and ordained you that ye should go and bring forth fruit and that your fruit should remain; that whatsoever ye shall ask of the Father in my name, He may give it you."

So, I did just that. I went out there and began picking the fruit and putting it in my shirt as I had folded it from the bottom. To my surprise, while I was busy picking the fruit and admiring the colors, some beautiful red strawberries appeared underneath all of the other fruit. (A red like I've never seen) I was then awakened out of the vision and I heard, "It's harvest time." I knew instantly that God wanted me to prepare to go to Water Valley to host a conference and reap the harvest there.

A few days later I had another vision that a first cousin of mine who lives in Water Valley also, told me that she had been trying to get in touch with me, because she wanted to tell me about her being on "this" machine but she never could tell me what type of machine she was referring to. So, I finally guessed life-support and she told me I was right. She told me she had been on life-support for over twenty years. Once again I was awakened and I asked the Lord what does this mean, as I knew she has never physically been on life-support at all, let alone for twenty years. He told me that "spiritually" she is barely hanging on by a string and that I needed to get to Water Valley to host a Healing and Deliverance Conference to help His people.

Well, I immediately began trying to get there in 2006, but I had no success in securing a building. Finally, in May 2007 as I was fasting and praying, the Lord revealed to me that the enemy had hindered me from entering that city. So, I redirected my prayers for that stronghold to be removed and destroyed completely! Within one hour, the city officials of Water Valley contacted me. They informed me that the first weekend in June 2007 was available to host the conference.

The Word says in Mark 9:29 "And he said unto them, this kind can come forth by nothing but by prayer and fasting." We must learn how to obey and apply the Word of God in our lives if we want to see change. So, Elder Bobby Sledge, his wife Amy, and many members of the Victory World Outreach Church of Huntsville went with me to carry out this conference. We witnessed an awesome move of God that weekend like never before!!!

At the people's request, we returned to Water Valley that same year in November 2007. After I finished preaching on Saturday morning, Elder Sledge laid hands on my daughter Paris and me.

Even though I know Elder Sledge possesses the five-fold ministry gifts, never did I think or believe that God was about to reveal and expose that "little girl" unto him this day in front of everyone! BUT, without warning and without my approval God did just that. These are the words I recall the Holy Spirit spoke through Elder Sledge unto me:

THE DAY I BEGAN TO "RISE ABOVE REJECTION"

"You have had walls up around you for years due to your pain. You have intentionally shut people out as you have tried to protect yourself and your feelings. You have wondered and asked God for years this same question over and over and that's "What's wrong with me?" That "little girl" has lived there inside so long and often manifested herself wanting to be loved and accepted. God says today, the walls will come down. He's going to answer your question TODAY and He says 'THERE IS NOTHING WRONG WITH YOU!' You are all right. You are all right."

Needless to say, I found myself completely bent over forward WEEPING and WAILING like I had n-e-v-e-r, e-v-e-r done even during the times I had cried privately. It was divinely clear to me that God had spoken, because I knew I had *never* shared this painful story with Elder Sledge or anyone there. I knew God and God alone had spoken this day and given me the *stamp of approval* that I had long sought after from so many others. I got totally and completely set free this day like you wouldn't believe. I literally felt "washing" and "cleansing" moving over my mind first and then my entire body. Why my mind first you might wonder? Well...because Evangelist Joyce Meyer says it best in the topic of one of her bestsellers, "The Battlefield of the Mind." That's where my battle and struggle with the "little girl" had been for all of these years. I needed a *new* mind.

All of the pain, hurt, feelings of abandonment, rejection, low self-esteem, self-hatred, depression, and suicidal thoughts had suffocated and saturated my thought patterns "in my mind." The cleansing stayed there on my mind a while and then it slowly moved down my entire body. I believe it was then. He was washing me of my past sins that were a result of my feelings of rejection.

A scripture comes to mind to explain to you how I felt. It is Ezekiel 36: 24-27 which says, "For I will take you from among the heathen, and gather you out of all countries and will bring you into your own land. Then will I sprinkle clean water upon you and ye shall be clean; from all your filthiness and from all your idols, will I cleanse you. A new heart also will I give you and a new spirit will I put within you; and I will take away the stony heart out of your flesh and I will give you an heart of flesh. And I will put my spirit within you and cause you to walk in my statues and ye shall keep my judgments and do *them*." When the Holy Spirit was done with me, I felt weightless in my mind and body. I not only felt brand new, but I felt like someone else altogether. I felt *clean and whole*. Most of all, I knew then, like never before, that there was absolutely nothing wrong with me from the perspective of why I had to live with grandma.

THAT'S JUST LIKE GOD!

Finally, if this wasn't mind-blowing enough, there's more. If you missed it earlier in the book, guess the geographical location where my *root of my rejection* took place? If you guessed Water Valley, you are right! My grandmother lived in Water Valley. Great and faithful is our GOD!! God took me *back* to the very location (physical root) where I first encountered rejection and ended it all there! HOW GREAT IS OUR GOD!!! I said early in the topic under self-hatred that we need to get up, wash ourselves, and fly back home. Little did I know that when God was showing me that I needed to go to Water Valley that my own complete healing from rejection and her relatives were dependent upon my obedience. Obedience truly is better than sacrifice. God didn't just want to use me to heal and deliver others, but He wanted me to experience that *same* healing and deliverance in my own life. Hallelujah! I have truly risen above my rejection because for the majority of my life, I lived under the spirit of rejection. It ruled my life, my actions and my behavior. As long as we are in the flesh, we will be in a war. If you don't agree, then please read Second Corinthians 4:8-9 which says, "We are troubled on every side, yet not distressed; we are perplexed, but not in despair; persecuted but not forsaken; cast down but not destroyed." Also, Paul talked about this battle in Romans 7:14-15 "For we know that the law is spiritual; but I am carnal, sold under sin. For that which I do I allow not; for what I would, that do I not; but what I hate, that do I." The answer to our constant defeat over rejection lies in our ability to recognize it, confront it, deal with it and denounce it from ever working again in our lives. Remember that "Death and life are in the power of the tongue; and they that love it shall eat the fruit thereof" according to Proverbs 18:21. Be cautious what you speak and allow others to speak over your life, your children, and all of those who are dear to you.

I thank God for allowing me to experience every painful thing that I've ever gone through in my entire life. The songwriter says, "Accept what God allows." For now, I am a much better woman. Psalms 119:71 says, "It's good for me that I have been afflicted, that I might learn thy statues." I can truly say like the songwriter Marvin Sapp, "I never would have made it without you (God). I'm stronger, I'm wiser, and I'm better, so much better. When I look back over all you've brought me through, I realize I made because I had you to hold on to." I believe that our past should be a place of reference only and not a place of residence. We all must learn to confront and handle our past and never let it handle us. Today and everyday I will RISE ABOVE REJECTION and from every negative emotion that hinders me from *flying high*. Why don't you make the same decree with me today?

> ## "I SHALL NOT DIE, BUT LIVE AND DECLARE THE WORKS OF THE LORD!!!"
> ### Psalms 118:17

I declare and decree in the NAME OF JESUS that each and every reader of this book will *immediately* begin to feel the healing power of God as He overtakes you and work out all of the pain in your heart and soul. I know God's Holy Spirit is delivering each reader, because otherwise, why was the enemy trying so desperately to get me to end my life *moments* before this divine revelation?

I live by this quotation, although the author is unknown. The words say:

"I SHALL PASS THROUGH THIS WORLD BUT ONCE.

IF THERE BE ANY KINDNESS I CAN SHOW OR ANY GOOD THING I CAN DO, LET ME DO IT NOW.

LET ME NOT DEFER IT NOR NEGLECT IT FOR I SHALL NOT PASS THIS WAY AGAIN"

ABOUT OUR MOTHER

I loved my Mother with everything in me.
And I still do even though she's deceased
now, because she sketched many beautiful
memories into my heart and soul. She
deposited seeds of wisdom and her voice
was one of reasoning. She would chastise
me if she thought or saw that I was
traveling wrong. She would often tell me
how proud she was of me and tell me to
go to college and finish. She would often
tell me that she didn't want my siblings or
me to ever have to work as hard as she
did.

She encouraged me to go overseas to play
professional basketball and she went to
the Canton High School track daily with
me to help me get in shape. As I jogged
by, I would hear her telling other ladies as
she walked with them that "that's my
baby and she's getting ready to go
overseas to play pro ball (mind you,
Renee was the baby)." I could hear the
joy in her voice and it made me proud
that she was my Mom. I later found out

she was terminally ill with cancer after I returned from Australia. It was revealed that she had been battling cancer since the 80's unknown to me and I believe my siblings as well, but that's just the way she desired it. I asked her why she didn't tell me *before* I left to go overseas. She told me because she wanted me to live my life and to not be worried about her. She always wanted each of us to go far in life. Our Mother was very, very funny and she *loved* to laugh and play jokes on you. And if you ever visited her for long, she was definitely going to challenge you in a game of Scrabble. She made us gather to play Scrabble and to sing gospel songs, as Beverly played the piano, a family tradition each holiday and anytime we got together.

To this day, all of my siblings and I stay up late nights challenging each other in a good game of Scrabble whenever we get together, whether it's just two of us or all seven of us. We even have our children begging to let them play now and most times we do. Mama truly started something with Scrabble. She could really sing also and she *loved* to sing!!! Joyce,

Beverly, my Mom and I sang in our church choir and my Mom led many of the songs. (I *tried* leading a couple) but Mama passed that gift to Renee. I recall when Beverly and I were young that we would go to Canton to visit her for the summers. Many times as we traveled back to Oxford for church on Sundays (which was a two-hour drive), she would start singing a song and wanted us to back her up. We would, but we had already planned to sing *loud and off beat* hoping she would tell us to be quiet, because we wanted to talk and play during that two-hour ride.

BUT to our surprise, she would backhand the both of us in the mouth at the same time (because I would be sitting in the middle on the front and I would catch her arm/elbow in the mouth as Bev got her hand in the mouth) and she'd tell us very emphatically, "don't *y'all* play with God!" Then she would tell us "now I'm getting ready to start over and *y'all* better sing and sing right this time. (I'm real tickled right now) As she started to sing again, we'd have to back her up with pain in our lips and she'd look at us laughing trying to keep singing while she knew we were mad and hurting.

She loved having all of her children at home for special holidays as she packed our spouses, our children, and us into her house at bedtime. She loved to cook and was great at it! I loved her sweet potato pies and her coconut cakes! She especially loved going to state fairs and carnivals and riding all the rides, eating cotton candy and candy apples even up in her latter years of life.

She would call us every October to let us know the State Fair was in Jackson, Mississippi and that we needed to come home and go with her. We did many of times. I recall how she would buy all of these tickets that hung down to the ground as we reached out our hands for the tickets thinking they were ours; she would tell us that those were all hers and we needed to purchase our own. (I'm smiling) So, we would purchase our tickets and try our best to keep up with her (even though we were grown) as she almost literally ran to each ride.

She taught me how to truly live life to its fullest! To not stress over the cares and issues of life! To not fear ANY people, but mainly ANY carnival rides. Mama departed this life on March 12, 1993 at the young age of fifty-four years. I love you Mama and look forward to seeing you again, as the elders use to say, "On that great get'n up moaning (morning)." (smiles)

ABOUT THE AUTHOR

VALERIE MARTIN-STEWART, **D. MIN. was born in Water Valley, Mississippi to the late Hervie Martin and the late Louise Martin-Pope. She was raised in Taylor, Mississippi by her uncle and aunt starting at the age of eight years old. She is divorced but was blessed with one beautiful daughter named Paris Marie from that marriage.**

PROFESSIONALLY, **Dr. Stewart has conducted many revivals, conferences, seminars, and traveled on the mission field nationally and internationally to include Peru and Jamaica. She is a sought-after motivational speaker at schools, churches, youth-at-risk facilities, and many government and non-government functions. She made her debut as a motivational speaker at the Blacks in Government (B.I.G.) National Training Conference in August 2007 when she conducted several workshops under the subject "Do It Afraid!" Dr. Stewart spoke profoundly to her listeners as she challenged them to step out of fear,** failure, and shame and tap into their true potential and follow their passions. She held four workshops and was asked by the committee members and participants to do more workshops that week. Her audience very well received her thought-provoking message. Her listeners rated her exceptionally high on the evaluation forms. She has been invited back to be a Workshop Presenter at the next B.I.G.'s Conference which will convene in New Orleans, August 2008.

She attended the 2007 Memphis Black Writer Conference in Memphis, Tennessee in May where she discussed her newly published book and how she overcame depression and rejection. She sat on a panel and shared her knowledge of how to publish a book. She held a book signing during the week of the conference. She has spoken at schools in February 2007 for Black History Month. She openly talked about her own life struggles, setbacks, and how she became self-motivated with God's help and rose above her circumstances. She challenged the audience to not be afraid to outshine others and fly high.

Ecclesiastically, Dr. Stewart was diversely raised under and sat at the sagacious feet of several renowned evangelical theologians, ministers, laity and seasoned educators. She accepted the Lord Jesus as her personal Savior at the young age of eight years old. She knew she was being called to preach at the age of sixteen years old, but ran from her calling for thirteen years as she had been raised in a strict Missionary Baptist church where she was taught that women were not called to preach, but to become missionaries only. She finally yielded to the Lord and accepted her calling in June 1997. She was licensed to preach in 1998 and ordained in 2000 both in the Cumberland Presbyterian Church.

EDUCATIONALLY, Dr. Stewart attended Lafayette High School in Oxford, Mississippi graduating with honors and in the top 5% of her class. She is listed in Who's Who among High School Students in the class of 1984. She matriculated for two years at Northwest Jr. College (NWJC) in Senatobia, Mississippi where she received her A.S. degree in Computer Science graduating with honors. She then matriculated at University of Alabama in Huntsville (UAH) where she received her B.S.E. degree in Electrical Engineering. She matriculated at Heritage Bible College and received her Masters in Biblical Studies, graduating Magna cum Laude with a 3.94 G.P.A. She matriculated to Andersonville Theological Seminary where she received her Doctorate in the Ministry also graduating Magna cum Laude with a 3.94 G.P.A. Dr. Stewart overcame her learning obstacles that she suffered in her earlier years, particularly being in remedial reading in junior high school. She is yet overcoming her shyness and fear of speaking in front of audiences.

ATHLETICALLY, Dr. Stewart played basketball, ran track, having earned many ribbons in high jump and mile relays, played softball and tennis in her junior high and High School years. She was blessed to receive athletic scholarships in basketball to NWJC and UAH. During her senior year in high school, she received the Tucker-Rowland Scholarship and The Craig Scholarship. She was the first recipient of the Tucker-

Rowland scholarship as one of her close friend and basketball teammate, "Shannon" and her sister Robin were both killed in a car accident in November 1983. Their parents began this scholarship Dr. Stewart's senior year as a memorial in the loss of their two daughters. Dr. Stewart received numerous awards in sports to include: Most Valuable Player, Best Defensive Player, and Player of the Week on numerous occasions. She was blessed to have the opportunity to play professional basketball in Peru, Australia, and toured in Italy. She was employed with the Australian Government as a Computer Analyst and Technical Support in two separate positions. Dr. Stewart was inducted into the University of Alabama in Huntsville Hall of Fame in February 1998 for her achievements in academics and athletics. She received a Bronze membership award.

JOURNALISTICALLY, Dr. Stewart has been writing for over twenty years starting at the young age of twelve. She became a published author on May 31, 2006 publishing her first book entitled

"Out of Pain Came Poetry" subtitled "Tapping into the Greatness Within." It's a collection of poems and writings, which mostly were written when she was suicidal.

PHILANTHROPICALLY, Dr. Stewart has timelessly enjoyed sharing her experiences, expertise and her resources with her hometown of Taylor, Mississippi, the surrounding cities, as well as abroad in other countries. She awards scholarships to the "C" & "D" average high school students who desires to attend college, university or a trade school. She was led by God to award the first two scholarships in August 2005 in her home church in Taylor out of her own personal resources. After having sown the first seed, she has been moved to tears by the many family, friends, and mostly strangers who have donated to the ministry so unselfishly. She has awarded students in Huntsville with the scholarship as well. She desires to award more scholarships in greater amounts. She has returned home to host revivals, conferences, and seminars for the youth and adults inspiring them with her words, time, talents and her heart, instilling in them that they have greatness within. In June 2005, God led her to start a non-profit outreach ministry entitled "Taking It By Force Outreach Ministries, Inc." based on Matthew 11:12. Dr. Stewart volunteers her time teaching weekly Bible Study at a "Youth-At- Risk" facility in Huntsville. She has hosted and was a featured speaker at a Grief Seminar to help those who were suffering the deaths of their children in the Lee High School bus tragedy. Scholarship donations were given to families in the loss of their daughters.

INTERNATIONALLY, Dr. Stewart traveled to Lima, Peru on a 10-day mission trip in June 2006 and to Montego Bay, Jamaica on a 7-day mission trip in April 2007 with Pastor Bruce Carter and the New Covenant Creations Ministries out of Alpharetta, Georgia. She had the opportunity to preach nightly, perform altar calls, visit and minister to the elderly as well as minister to children at many girls and boys orphanages. She was invited back to Jamaica to do a Women's Conference and preach a Crusade by two local pastors there. Dr. Stewart returned to Montego Bay to preach a Crusade and do mission work with a team under her own ministry, "Taking It By Force Outreach Ministries, Inc." in October 2007. She spoke at several Jamaican schools motivating the youth. Once again, she has been invited back to preach more crusades. She plans to return to Montego Bay in 2008.

As an Ordained Minister, Professional/Motivational Speaker, Electrical Engineer, Published and Noted Author, Founder of a Non-profit ministry, and former world class athlete,

Dr. Stewart is available to do training and keynote speaking at conventions, companies, federal and state-sponsored events, civic associations, for school systems, and at churches. To make a donation to the ministry or learn more about her speaking availability and seminar schedules as well as her resources, contact her via phone at 256.726.9986, on her website at www.valeriemstewart.com or via e-mail at vstewart@knology.net.

Printed in the United States
115470LV00002B/325-645/P